Ulysses S. Grant

Wendy Conklin, M.A.

Table of Contents

Who Was This Man?

His drive to finish a job helped him win the Civil War. His fight to win battles made him a hero. He was president of the United States even though he was not a good **politician** (pol-uh-TISH-uhn). From a poor home to West Point, from the battlefield to the White House, he did it all. He was Ulysses S. Grant.

Grant's graduation ▶ from West Point

Ulysses S. Grant

Lyss, the Boy

Hiram Ulysses Grant was born in 1822 in a small town in Ohio. Grant did not like his real name. Classmates teased him because his initials (in-ISH-uhlz) spelled HUG. Other kids called him "Useless" instead of Ulysses. When he was a boy, his friends and family nicknamed him Lyss.

As a young man, he found work as a **tanner** in his father's shop. But the blood on the animal hides made him sick. So, his father hoped Grant would enter the military.

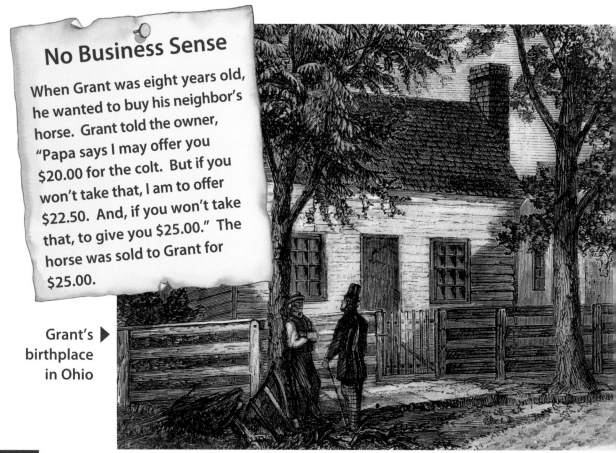

No Business Sense

When Grant was eight years old, he wanted to buy his neighbor's horse. Grant told the owner, "Papa says I may offer you $20.00 for the colt. But if you won't take that, I am to offer $22.50. And, if you won't take that, to give you $25.00." The horse was sold to Grant for $25.00.

Grant's ▶ birthplace in Ohio

To succeed in the military, young men went to West Point Military Academy. It was hard to get into West Point. Each student had to have a **recommendation** (rek-uh-men-DAY-shuhn) from a congressman. The congressman who wrote the letter for Grant made a mistake. He called Grant, Ulysses Simpson Grant. From then on, Grant was known as U.S. Grant or Ulysses S. Grant.

◀ Buildings at West Point Military Academy

▼ This map shows the river that flows near West Point.

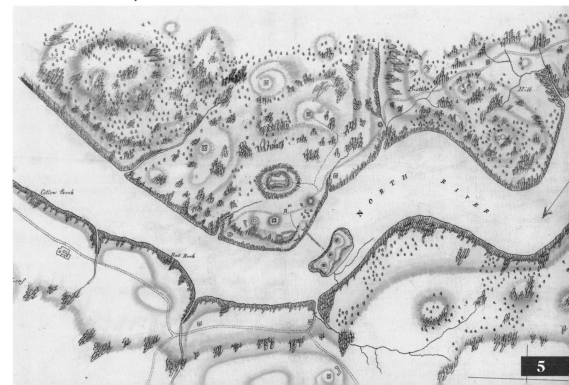

Grant in Mexico

After graduating from West Point, the army sent Grant to fight in Mexico. The United States was fighting a war with Mexico. The two countries could not agree on the borders of Texas.

It did not take Grant long to understand the **strategy** (STRAT-uh-gee) of war. In one attack, Grant rode through heavy fighting to get more **ammunition** (am-yuh-NISH-uhn). He made a shield by strapping himself to one side of his horse. His horse protected him from the Mexican bullets.

Later, Grant faced a large group of Mexicans. He and his men dragged a cannon into the bell tower of a church. They aimed the cannon at their enemy and fired. This was a great victory for Grant and the Americans. Even people in Washington, D.C., heard about Grant's success.

◀ **Grant firing a cannon at the enemy**

Love and Marriage

After the war, Grant married his friend's sister, Julia Dent. They both shared a love for horses. In fact, Grant was known for his riding at West Point.

▲ Julia Dent Grant

Lieutenant Grant during ▶
the Mexican War

Beyond the War

After the war, the army transferred Grant to the West Coast. He wanted to have his wife and children there with him. So, he tried to make some quick money so they could join him. He put all his cash into opening a store with a friend. The friend took advantage of Grant and left him penniless. Next, Grant tried running a **billiard** (BIL-yuhrd) **parlor,** but it also failed. Grant began drinking alcohol. He was sad and lonely.

When an officer discovered him drunk, Grant faced a **court-martial** (MAR-shuhl). He resigned from the army. Grant's father was very upset about this. He asked the **secretary of war** for help. Even the secretary of war, a man named Jefferson Davis, would not put Grant back in the army.

▼ Grant's family was very important to him.

Jefferson Davis

The In-between Years

After failing as a farmer, Grant returned to his father's **tannery** (TAN-uh-ree) for a job. His father hired him as a clerk, but Grant was not good at remembering prices. While on the job, Grant spent most of his time studying Napoleon's war in France.

▼ Grant studied the war strategies of Napoleon Bonaparte.

Signing Up for Service Again

Grant wanted to serve in the army again. This time, he wanted to be in command. He wrote a letter to leaders in Washington, D.C. But, they ignored his letter. Then, he tried to meet with military leaders. These men knew that Grant had a drinking problem. They would not even talk with him.

Finally, the governor of Illinois told Grant to report for duty. He ordered Grant to command the 21st Illinois Volunteers. These volunteers were rowdy men. Grant knew he had his work cut out for him.

▼ **Grant drilling the 21st Illinois Volunteers**

When the men saw Grant in his worn-out clothes, they made fun of him. They could not believe he would be their commander. In no time at all, Grant had them in shape and practicing drills. The Civil War had begun. These men were ready to go to war.

Who Fought the War?

The Civil War was fought between the North and the South. Soldiers in the South were called Confederates or rebels. Northerners were called Yankees or Union soldiers.

▼ Grant was very comfortable on horseback.

Serving Under General Halleck

At the beginning of the Civil War, Grant served for the Union under General Henry Halleck. Before each battle, Grant had to get his plans approved. General Halleck did not like the way Grant ignored orders while in battle. So, Halleck made Grant's army wait around for months. Halleck ignored or denied every plan that Grant had.

In February 1862, Halleck let Grant attack Fort Donelson in Tennessee. Southern soldiers held this fort. At first, the Confederates (kuhn-FED-uhr-uhtz) were winning the battle. Then, the Confederates got confused about their orders. Grant attacked and recovered the lost ground.

General Henry Halleck ▶

▲ Battle of Fort Donelson

The Confederate general asked Grant about **terms of surrender** (suh-REN-duhr). Grant replied, "No terms except an **unconditional** (uhn-kuhn-DISH-uh-nuhl) and immediate surrender can be accepted!" This meant Grant wanted the Confederates to completely give up the battlefield.

The enemy **surrendered** and Grant captured 15,000 prisoners and 4,000 horses. This was the first big victory for the North in the Civil War.

U. S. Grant

Grant's words to the Confederate general spread throughout the North. Northerners took his initials and changed his name to "Unconditional Surrender" Grant. Grant was promoted to major general because of this victory.

▲ **Fighting at the Battle of Shiloh**

Bloody Shiloh

In April 1862, Grant's army was still in Tennessee. Grant and his men were camped near Shiloh. They were there drilling to prepare new **recruits** for the war. Unknown to Grant, the southern army was very close. They were planning a surprise attack on the Union army.

When the battle broke out, Union men ran for their lives. They were scared and tried to get away from the gunfire. General Grant mounted his horse and rode among his troops. He rallied them to continue fighting. They fought all day and into the night. By the end of the first day of the battle, Grant's men were exhausted.

The next day, new troops arrived to help the Union. But a Confederate attack from the side surprised them again. Grant yelled, "Advance and recapture our original camp!" His men followed him and pushed back their enemy.

The armies of the North and the South lost more than 10,000 men each. The Battle of Shiloh was one of the worst battles in United States history.

▲ Grant and his officers on horseback

That Jealous Halleck!

Grant's problems with General Halleck were not over yet. After the bloody battle at Shiloh, Halleck spoke with President Abraham Lincoln. Halleck blamed the large loss of northern lives on Grant's drinking problem.

Victory in Vicksburg

Beginning in April 1863, Grant moved toward Vicksburg, Mississippi. Vicksburg was very important to the South. Forces at Vicksburg controlled the Mississippi River. President Abraham Lincoln believed that Vicksburg was the key to winning the war.

Attacking Vicksburg was not an easy task. The Confederates had many soldiers throughout Mississippi. Their job was to keep the Union soldiers away from Vicksburg. Throughout April and May, Grant's army faced Confederate troops.

On May 19, Grant finally reached Vicksburg. He tried two assaults on the forces at Vicksburg. After losing 4,000 men, Grant realized attacking the city would not work. It was too well protected.

▼ Grant's army used pontoon bridges to cross the rivers in Mississippi.

Instead, Grant's army dug **trenches** around Vicksburg. The Union army cut Vicksburg off from supplies and communicating with the rest of the country. The **siege** (SEEJ) was successful. People in the city almost starved. After 47 days, the city surrendered. This victory divided the South and gave the North control of the Mississippi River.

Mule for Dinner

The people and soldiers in Vicksburg were so hungry, they ate their mules and horses.

▼ Fighting near Vicksburg, Mississippi

Commanding the Army

In March 1864, President Lincoln put Grant in charge of the entire northern army. Grant did not want the war to continue much longer. The longer it went, the more lives would be lost.

One of the first things he did was stop **prisoner exchanges** between the North and South. The South's army was much smaller than the Union army. There were many southern prisoners in northern prisons. The South could not afford to fight much longer because they did not have enough men.

▼ President Lincoln named Grant the commander of the Union army in 1864.

▼ Lincoln promoted Grant to lieutenant general in March 1864.

Executive Mansion,
Washington, D.C.,
March 10th 1864.

Under the authority of the act of Congress to revive the grade of Lieutenant General in the United States Army, approved February 29th 1864, Lieutenant General Ulysses S. Grant, U.S. Army, is assigned to the command of the armies of the United States.

Abraham Lincoln

▲ The armies fought the Battle of the Wilderness as the Northerners got close to Richmond, Virginia.

Passing Notes

Grant and Lee sometimes exchanged notes. They told each other that they knew what the other had for breakfast or dinner. This was their way of saying they had spies in each other's camps.

Grant had a plan for how to win the war. He wanted to attack and **occupy** (OCK-yuh-pie) big cities in the South. General William Sherman marched through the Deep South. He launched "Total War" on the Southerners there. That meant that he destroyed the land and cities as he marched through. Without support from home, Sherman and Grant thought the southern army would give up.

In Virginia, Grant's army clashed with General Robert E. Lee's army. Little by little, Grant made his way to the southern capital in Richmond.

The End in Sight

From June 1864 to April 1865, the two armies faced each other near Petersburg, Virginia. Petersburg is just south of Richmond. Grant dug trenches and laid siege to the city.

Grant did not think that he could break through the Confederate lines at Petersburg. So, he secretly had coal miners dig a tunnel. This tunnel stretched all the way to Lee's army. The Northerners filled the tunnel with dynamite and lit the fuse.

The explosion sent dirt, men, and guns everywhere. A huge crater opened up and Grant's men charged into it. Lee's men ran to the top edge and fired down on the Union forces. More than 4,000 Union soldiers died. Grant knew he had made a huge mistake.

This ▶ engraving shows the battle lines around Petersburg.

◀ Lee surrendering to Grant at Appomattox Court House

However, Lee's army could not survive the siege much longer. They left Petersburg and lost control of their capital at Richmond. In April 1865, Lee wrote a note to Grant. The two leaders agreed to meet in Appomattox (ap-uh-MAT-uhks) Court House, Virginia. Lee surrendered the southern army to Grant. The war was over.

The Presidency

After the war, Grant was a hero. Everyone wanted to meet him. In 1868, he was elected president of the United States. But, Grant was not a politician, he was a war hero. He did not know the first thing about running a country.

His years as president were filled with **scandals**. Grant had good intentions, but he trusted people too much. Wealthy men took advantage of him. He was relieved when his two terms ended.

▲ President Grant delivered his second inaugural address on March 4, 1873.

Mark Twain

▼ Grant writing his memoirs

The American author Mark Twain convinced Grant to write his **memoirs** (MEM-warz). Grant wrote about everything from childhood to his years in the army. He finished his book one week before dying of throat cancer in 1885. His book was an instant best seller.

People around the world wanted to know more about Grant. He was a puzzle to people. How could he be so successful in war and so unsuccessful everywhere else? Ulysses S. Grant will always be remembered as a great general who helped save the Union.

A Hero's Welcome

After his two terms as president, Grant and his wife traveled the world. Everywhere they went people welcomed him as a hero.

Glossary

ammunition—supply of bullets and shells for guns or cannons

billiard parlor—a place where people can play pool

Confederates—people who supported the South in the Civil War; comes from the name of the country formed by the states that suceded, the Confederate States of America

court-martial—a trial for someone in the military

memoirs—autobiographical stories

occupy—to take control

pardon—to excuse from any punishment

politician—a person who runs for and serves in a political office

prisoner exchanges—when the North and South traded prisoners of war

recommendation—an oral or written expression describing someone in a positive way

recruits—new soldiers in the military

scandals—behaviors that lead to people thinking you have low moral values

secretary of war—the person in charge of all aspects of the military under the president

siege—a military blockade of an area that cuts off all contact with the outside world

strategy—the planning of a military attack

surrendered—gave up and lost a battle or the war

tanner—someone who works with animal hides

tannery—a place where animal hides are turned into leather

terms of surrender—the agreement for accepting surrender

treason—when someone attempts to overthrow a government or does something that harms his or her country

trenches—long ditches in the ground

unconditional—absolute and without any limits

Union—term used to describe the United States of America; also the name given to the northern army during the Civil War

FOUR DOORS, THREE TRAPS

There are four doors to choose from, but only one will reveal the secret passageway out of the tomb. The other routes are riddled with traps and lead to dead ends! Which door should you choose? As you stand in front of them, you notice that each one has a different symbol on it ...

Hey, one of them matches the symbol on the map!

Each symbol is a top-down view of a pyramid.

 **EGYPT FACT**

Ancient Egyptians were big fans of board games. Their version of dice were called "knuckle bones" or "throw sticks."

Your challenge is to figure out which symbol matches the pyramid on the map.

CHALLENGE RATING

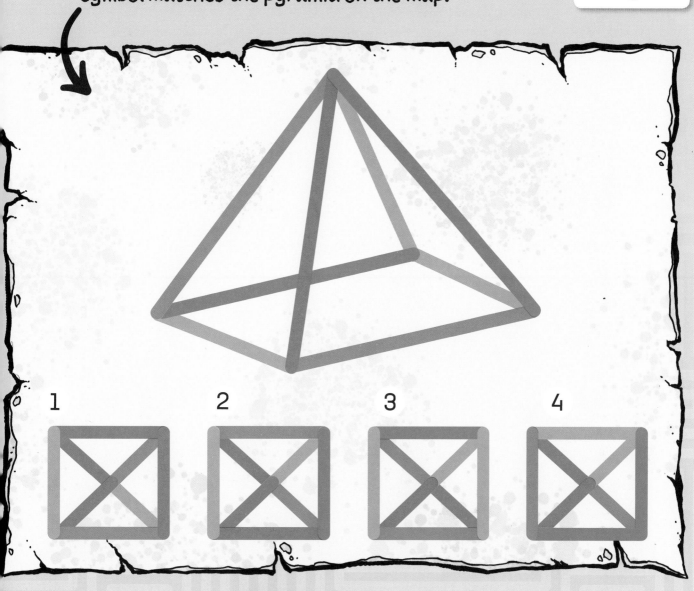

1   2   3   4

You did it!

You open the doorway with the matching symbol and walk through it. Inside, the passageway is dark and winding, but you can see a light in the distance.

51

SKETCH IT!

You all frantically scramble down the passageway toward the light and emerge in what appears to be the treasury. Zane grabs his sketchbook and excitedly starts doodling a set of canopic jars he has spotted. Grab a pencil and get drawing to make his sketch match the scene exactly!

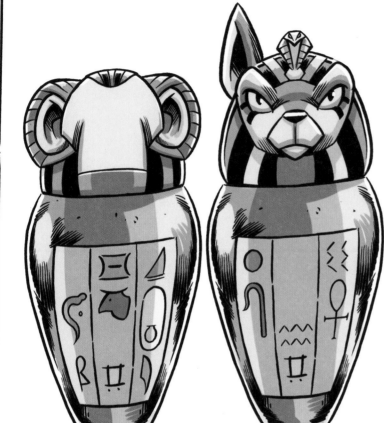

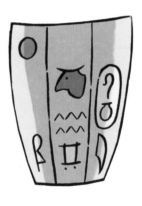

These are incredible. I have to sketch them!

My app might be able to translate those hieroglyphs!

Be quick!

As Zane draws, Cassia studies the hieroglyphs on one of the canopic jars and quickly scans them into her device ...

ANAGRAM ANTICS

As soon as Cassia has scanned the hieroglyphs, her app brings up a series of anagrams. Suddenly, you hear a mysterious ticking noise start up from somewhere in the room. It's a race against the clock to rearrange the words. Too slow and all the letters will disappear! Can you help the team solve this?

Hint

Each word has an ancient Egyptian theme!

We need to rearrange these letters into words before we can go any further.

1. oharahp

2. shpnix

3. rseature

4. rhinse

5. dyrapmi

6. dgdesos

1 _____

2 _____

3 _____

4 _____

5 _____

6 _____

Fill in your answers here!

Cracked it!

You solve the final anagram, and then a message appears on Cassia's tablet: *"Rearrange the tiles to discover who is hidden ..."*

EGYPT FACT

The ancient Egyptians worshipped over 2,000 gods and goddesses. Many of them were depicted as humans with animal heads.

JUMBLED DISGUISE

After searching high and low, Kiran eventually finds a portrait of a goddess made from tiles on a far wall—but some of the tiles are missing! You look around and see that a number of tiles have fallen to the floor. Can you figure out which ones fit the gaps?

Write the correct letters in the spaces to complete the portrait.

Good luck!

Alrighty, let's work out which tiles fit where.

Awesome!

The goddess portrait was disguising the exit all along. As you slide the final tile into place, the portrait parts to reveal four more doors.

EGYPT FACT

Not all ancient Egyptians were mummified. It was very expensive and took a long time, so it was only for the richest people.

BLOCKED OUT

Each door has a number painted on it, along with a picture of some blocks. But how does that help you? On the correct door, the number at the top should match the number of blocks in the picture—that's the door you need!

Ha! Ha! Ha!

Did you hear about the stressed-out mummy? He was all wound up!

Beep, beep!

Cassia's app begins to make a beeping noise—it's the reminder she set, meaning your classmates are due to leave the tomb in five minutes! Go, go, go!

UNRAVELING

As you rush hastily through the correct door, you fall into a tangle of unraveling mummy bandages. Yikes! Your task is to find which one leads you out of this room and back to your classmates.

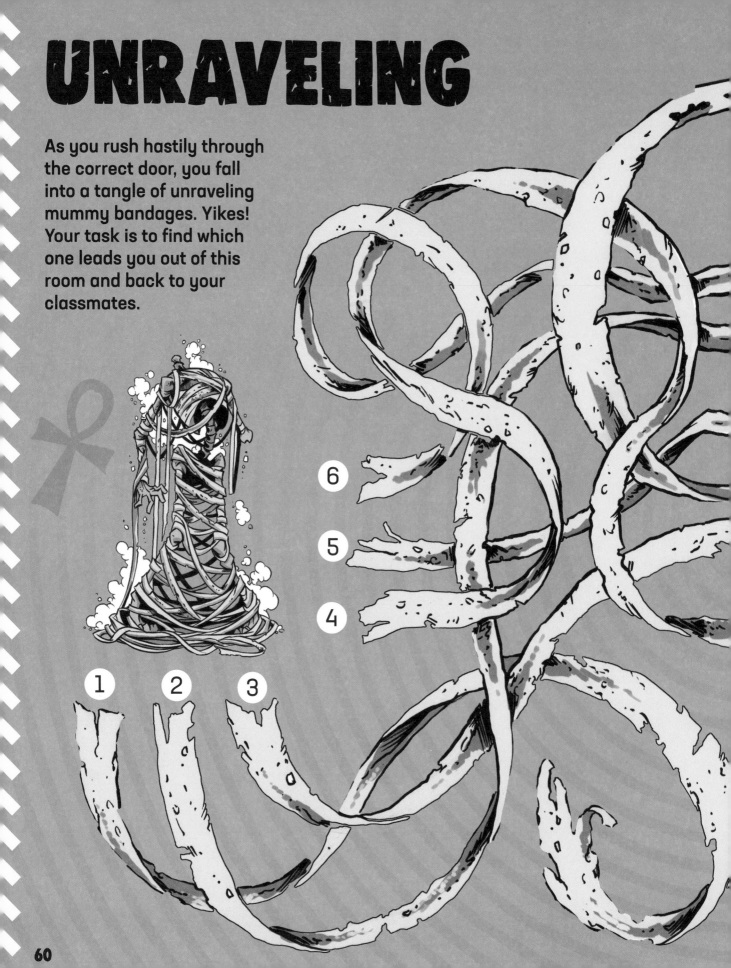

ANSWERS

PAGES 10-11
1: TOP LINE: **5, 3**
   BOTTOM LINE: **4, 3**

2: TOP LINE: **1**
   RIGHT LINE: **3**
   BOTTOM LINE: **3, 10**

3: TOP LINE: **2, 4**
   RIGHT LINE: **5**
   BOTTOM LINE: **10**

PAGES 12-13

PAGES 14-15

PAGES 18-19
1: **18**   2: **10**   3: **26**

PAGES 20-21

PAGES 22-23

PAGES 24-25

PAGES 28-29
The answer is 30

PAGES 30-31
The answer is 20

PAGES 32-33
A: **2**   B: **1**   C: **6**

PAGES 34-35

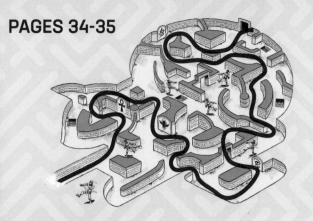

PAGES 36-37

PAGES 40-41

8 + 5 1 6 ⬆

PAGES 42-43

PAGES 44-45

The correct order for the
alarms is: 3 7 8 9

PAGES 46-47

1: **Q**   2: **A**   3: **I**   4: **J**   5: **O**   6: **K**
7: **M**   8: **H**   9: **R**   10: **B**

PAGES 50-51

The answer is 3

PAGES 54-55

1: **pharaoh**
2: **sphinx**
3: **treasure**
4: **shrine**
5: **pyramid**
6: **goddess**

PAGES 56-57

A: **4**   B: **9**   C: **8**   D: **2**

PAGES 58-59

This is the correct door

PAGES 60-61

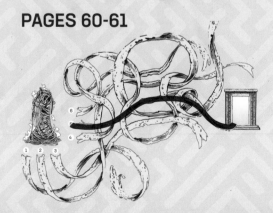

SEE YOU ON THE NEXT ADVENTURE!

Color in the team!